CONFIDENT

IN A

JUDGMENTAL

WORLD

NOTE TO READERS

This manuscript supports learning and personal growth. It does not replace medical or mental health care. If a reader feels unsafe, overwhelmed for a long time, or has thoughts of self-harm, please tell a trusted adult and seek professional help promptly.

CONTENTS

CHAPTER 1 - Confidence Under the Spotlight

Some days, life feels like a scoreboard. There are points for grades, points for tryouts, points for being "cool," and points for what people say online. Even if nobody is holding a clipboard, your brain can act like it is being watched.

When the world feels judge-y, it is easy to mix up two things: being evaluated and being valued. Evaluation is about a result in one moment. Value is about who you are. Those are not the same.

Confidence is not the same as never getting hurt. Confidence is the steady belief that you can handle what comes next. It is quiet. It is practical. And it can be built.

Here is a common scene. You get a test back. The number is lower than you hoped. Your stomach drops. Your mind rushes to a big sentence: "I'm not smart." Or you see friends doing something without you, and the sentence becomes: "Nobody wants me."

Those big sentences feel real, but they are usually stories, not facts. A fact is small and clear: "I got 72%." "I was not invited." A story is a meaning your brain adds: "This proves I'm behind forever." "This means I don't belong."

Your brain tells stories for a reason. It wants to protect you. If it predicts something bad, it thinks you will prepare. But when the story is too harsh, it does not help you prepare. It makes you freeze, hide, or give up. That is how confidence shrinks.

A strong mind learns to separate the two voices: the Reporter voice and the Story voice. The Reporter voice says what happened. The Story voice guesses what it means. You need both voices, but you do not have to let the Story voice drive the whole bus.

When you bring the Reporter voice back, the pressure gets smaller. You can say, "I missed these questions," instead of, "I'm a failure." You can say, "I feel left out," instead of, "I will always be alone." Feelings matter, but they do not get to write your whole future.

Now we can talk about the parts of confidence. Think of confidence like a three-part shield. The first part is worth. The second is skills. The third is direction.

Worth means your basic value does not change with a grade, a comment, or a mistake. You can be disappointed and still be worthy. If you would not call a friend "trash" for one bad day, you do not have to call yourself that either.

Skills mean you can get better. Confidence grows faster when you collect real proof: practice that improved something, study that made a topic clearer, a brave moment where you spoke up, a hard day where you kept going.

Direction means you know what matters to you. It could be kindness, curiosity, teamwork, honesty, or learning. When you know your values, you make choices that fit you, not choices that only chase approval.

Here is the good news: evaluation does not have to be the enemy. A score can be information. Feedback can be a map.

2

People can have opinions, and you can still keep your inner balance.

If you have a trusted adult, use them like a teammate. You do not need a lecture. You need steadiness. A helpful adult can remind you: "This is a moment, not a label."

Confidence under the spotlight is not about shining brighter than everyone else. It is about staying real while you grow. The world may keep ranking and commenting, but your life can belong to you.

CHAPTER 2 - Comparison and the Online Mirror

Comparison is a normal human habit. Your brain notices where you are and where other people are, the way a map notices distance. Sometimes that helps. It can show you what is possible and teach you new ideas. But comparison can also turn into a heavy kind of math: it starts counting your worth as if you were a score.

For kids and teens, comparison feels louder because life is already full of measuring. School has grades and levels. Sports have tryouts and rankings. Friend groups have invitations, jokes, and quiet signals about who belongs. When you add the internet, comparison can follow you home and sit on your pillow.

An online feed is often called a mirror, but it is not a flat mirror. It is more like a funhouse mirror that stretches some parts and hides others. It shows highlights, not the whole story. It shows the good angle, not the messy day. It shows the moment after the hard work, not the hours of practice. If you compare your real life to someone else's highlights, your brain will feel behind even when you are doing fine.

Imagine a student named Kai. Kai posts one photo after a great day. Friends comment with emojis and compliments. Someone else sees it and thinks, "Kai is always having fun. Kai is always confident." But Kai's great day is one day. The unseen days include boredom, worries, and mistakes—just like everyone else.

Comparison becomes most painful when it forgets context. Context includes effort, time, resources, health, family, and luck.

Two people can be the same age and live in totally different situations. That does not make one person "better." It makes the comparison unfair.

There is another reason comparison stings: it often steals attention from your own growth. When you stare at someone else's page, you stop reading your own progress. You may not notice that you are braver than last month, kinder than last year, or stronger than you were before. Growth is quiet. Comparison is loud.

A steadier kind of confidence uses comparison differently. Instead of asking, "Am I above or below?" it asks, "What can I learn?" If you admire someone's drawing, you can notice the skill, not the status. If you admire someone's running speed, you can notice the training, not the rank. Learning comparison turns jealousy into curiosity. It keeps your self-respect intact.

Sometimes comparison is really a clue about values. You might feel a sting when you see someone being included, because belonging matters to you. You might feel a sting when you see someone win, because achievement matters to you. The sting is not proof that you are small. It is proof that something matters. Values are not enemies. They are signals.

The online world makes values noisy because it rewards attention. The most extreme moments get the most clicks. The most perfect-looking bodies get the most likes. The most dramatic stories get shared the fastest. This can trick your brain into thinking that "more attention" means "more worth." It does not. Attention is not love. Popularity is not safety. A strong life is built in quiet places too.

A helpful rule is this: your feelings deserve respect, but not every feeling deserves to lead. If scrolling makes you feel smaller, that is information. It does not mean you are weak. It means your mind is hungry for something more real. Real things include sleep, movement, talking with someone who cares, making something with your hands, and being with people who see you clearly.

When you cannot avoid comparison, you can still choose where to place your eyes. You can choose role models who make you want to grow without hating yourself. You can choose friends who celebrate your wins without turning everything into a contest. You can choose to be the kind of person who does not compete for worth.

Confidence in a judgmental world does not mean you stop noticing other people. It means you stop using other people as a ruler for your value. Your life is not a race against your friends. It is a path you walk at your own pace, with your own goals, and your own kindness.

CHAPTER 3 - Feedback Without Shame

Feedback is everywhere. Teachers correct work. Coaches point out mistakes. Parents give reminders. Friends react to what you say. Some feedback is gentle. Some is sharp. Some is confusing. The problem is not that feedback exists. The problem is what your mind does with it.

Many young people make the same mistake: they turn feedback into a verdict about who they are. A comment about a paper becomes, "I'm dumb." A correction in practice becomes, "I'm terrible." A parent's frustration becomes, "I disappoint everyone." This is not feedback anymore. This is shame.

Shame is the feeling that says, "Something is wrong with me." It makes you want to hide. It makes you want to disappear. It can feel like a heavy coat you cannot take off. Shame is not a useful teacher. It does not show you the next step. It only pushes you away from learning.

There is a healthier way to hold feedback. It begins with a simple separation: a note about performance is not a statement about personhood. A teacher can say, "Your paragraph needs clearer evidence," and you can still be a smart, good, worthy human being. A coach can say, "Your form is off," and you can still be an athlete who is improving.

Imagine a student named Mira. Mira gets a test back with marks in red. Mira's cheeks burn. The mind shouts, "Everyone can see I failed." The body wants to crumple the paper. But the red marks are not a spotlight. They are a map. They show where Mira lost points so Mira can find the path back.

Helpful feedback is usually specific. It names what happened and what could change. It is about the work, not about your worth. Unhelpful feedback is vague, insulting, or dramatic. It sounds like, "What's wrong with you?" or "You never listen." Unhelpful feedback does not deserve to live in your head for free.

Sometimes the same sentence can feel helpful or harmful depending on the tone. That is why confidence needs an inner filter. A filter does not mean you ignore everything. It means you sort. You keep what can help you grow. You release what is only meant to hurt.

One calm way to sort feedback is to translate it into a next step. Next steps are small and concrete. "Practice this one move slowly." "Add one example to this paragraph." "Ask one question when you do not understand." When feedback becomes a next step, shame has less room to spread.

Sometimes feedback is unfair. Sometimes adults are tired. Sometimes peers are rude. When that happens, your job is not to prove your worth to the loudest voice. Your job is to protect your inner respect and bring the situation to a safer place. That might mean asking for clarity, taking a break, or involving a trusted adult. Strength is not always arguing. Strength is also choosing a better setting.

A confident person can say, "I hear the correction," without saying, "I am the problem." They can say, "I can improve," without saying, "I am not enough." This is the difference between growth and humiliation. Growth keeps dignity. Humiliation steals dignity.

It also helps to remember that feelings rise fast and fall slowly. When feedback lands, the first wave can feel huge. Give your body time. Breathing, water, a walk, or a quiet minute can calm the alarm system inside you. When the alarm quiets down, your brain becomes smarter again.

Feedback is part of learning. You do not need to love it, but you can learn to use it without breaking yourself. If you can stay kind to yourself while being corrected, you will be powerful in school, in sports, in friendships, and later in work. That kind of power is not loud. It is steady.

CHAPTER 4 - Purpose That Outlasts Grades

Grades can matter, but grades cannot hold your whole life. A grade measures one performance at one time. It cannot measure your kindness. It cannot measure your courage. It cannot measure what you will become.

When life feels like one long report card, it is easy to forget the reason behind the work. You study to avoid trouble, to avoid disappointment, to avoid feeling "less than." That kind of studying is heavy. It can make learning feel like a punishment instead of a power.

Purpose is the part of you that remembers "why." It does not have to be dramatic. It does not have to be a big dream. Purpose can be small and real: learning because you like understanding things, practicing because you want to be reliable on a team, reading because you want words that help you think, helping because you want people around you to feel safe.

Imagine a student named Lila who loves building things. Lila can take apart a toy and put it back together. But Lila starts thinking that only top grades count, so Lila stops building and only chases numbers. After a while, Lila feels tired and empty. The numbers keep moving, but the joy is gone.

Purpose brings the joy back, not by removing effort, but by giving effort a direction. It reminds you that skills are not only for school. Skills are for life. Communication helps friendships. Math helps planning. Reading helps imagination. Practice helps patience. When learning connects to life, it feels less like pressure and more like growth.

A helpful picture is a compass. A compass does not tell you every step, but it tells you which way is north. Purpose is your north. It helps you choose when choices are hard. It helps you keep going when results are slow.

Purpose also protects confidence. If your only purpose is "be the best," then any setback feels like a threat. But if your purpose includes character—being brave, being honest, being kind—then a setback becomes a lesson, not a collapse. You can be proud of how you act, even when the score is not what you wanted.

Purpose can live in your values. Values are the kind of person you want to be. Some kids value curiosity. Some value teamwork. Some value creativity. Some value fairness. Values do not need permission from the internet. They do not need approval from a crowd. They belong to you.

When you know your values, you can set goals that fit your life. A goal is not only a number. A goal can be a habit: practicing ten minutes, finishing homework with focus, asking for help when stuck, speaking honestly in a friendship, being a person who tries again.

This does not mean grades are meaningless. It means grades are not the boss of your identity. You can care about results and still care about your heart. You can want improvement without treating yourself like a machine.

A purpose-filled life makes room for rest as well. Rest is not laziness. Rest is fuel. When you rest, your brain stores learning, your body repairs, and your emotions settle. Purpose does not demand endless pushing. Purpose includes wise recovery.

When you build purpose, you build a future that cannot be taken away by one bad day. You become someone who is learning for life, not performing for a score. That is the kind of confidence that lasts.

CHAPTER 5 - Resilience in Real Life

Resilience is the skill of returning. It is not being unbreakable. It is not pretending you do not care. Resilience is what happens after a hard moment, when you find your feet again.

Kids often imagine resilient people as tough and emotionless. But real resilience includes feelings. A resilient person can feel sad and still show up. They can feel embarrassed and still learn. They can feel angry and still choose a respectful action.

Imagine a student named Noah who misses an easy question on a test. Noah feels hot embarrassment. The mind wants to erase the mistake by erasing the whole day. The body wants to quit trying. This is the moment where resilience begins—not with a perfect thought, but with a small return to steadiness.

Resilience has two parts: recovery and re-entry. Recovery is how you calm your body and mind. Re-entry is how you step back into life without letting fear control you. Some people recover but never re-enter. They hide. Others re-enter without recovering, and they explode. A balanced person learns both.

Recovery can be quiet. It can look like drinking water, taking a shower, sitting in a calm place, or talking to someone safe. It can look like saying, "That was hard," without adding, "So I am hopeless." Naming the feeling honestly is not weakness. It is accuracy.

Re-entry is also quiet. It is choosing the next doable step. After a bad grade, re-entry might be asking what was missed and studying that part. After a friendship problem, re-entry might be repairing with a message that is simple and sincere. After a loss in sports, re-entry might be returning to practice and focusing on one skill.

Resilience grows when you practice small discomforts on purpose. Not big, dramatic suffering—small, ordinary challenges. Finishing a draft even when it is not perfect. Raising your hand even when your voice shakes. Trying again after a mistake. These moments teach your nervous system a powerful truth: discomfort is survivable.

Resilience also grows with support. A strong person is not a person who needs nobody. A strong person knows where to get help. Trusted adults, kind friends, coaches, teachers, and family members can be part of your support team. Asking for help is not cheating. It is wisdom.

One enemy of resilience is the belief that mistakes are dangerous. If mistakes feel dangerous, you will avoid them, and avoidance will shrink your world. But mistakes are part of learning. They are information. They show what to practice next.

Another enemy is harsh self-talk. Harsh self-talk sounds like a bully living in your head. It says things you would never say to a younger kid. A more resilient inner voice sounds like a steady coach: truthful, firm, and kind. It says, "That hurt. Now we take the next step."

Resilience does not erase your need for rest. When you are tired, your feelings get louder and your patience gets smaller. Sleep, food, movement, and play are not "extra." They are part of the foundation. A tired brain has trouble being brave. A rested brain can return more easily.

In a judgmental world, resilience protects your confidence. The world can comment, rank, and compare, but you learn that you can come back. You can rebuild. You can keep going. That knowledge becomes a quiet strength you carry into every new challenge.

CHAPTER 6 - When Your Body Panics

Sometimes confidence disappears for a surprising reason: your body gets there first. Your heart races. Your stomach flips. Your hands feel sweaty. Your thoughts speed up like a bike going downhill.

When that happens, it is easy to think, "I'm weak," or "I can't handle this." But a racing heart is not a character flaw. It is a body system doing its job too loudly.

Your body has an alarm system. It was built to keep you safe. If it senses danger, it tries to help by giving you extra energy. That is why your breathing changes and your muscles tighten.

The problem is that the alarm system is not great at telling the difference between a tiger and a test, between a real threat and a social moment. It reacts fast, and sometimes it reacts to things that are scary but not dangerous.

You might feel the alarm before a presentation, before a tryout, before asking a question in class, or before walking into a room where you worry people will judge you. The fear feels like a rule: "Stop." But fear is not always a rule. Sometimes fear is just a signal that you care.

A calm kind of confidence begins with understanding this: your feelings are real, and they are also temporary. They rise, peak, and fall, like a wave. If you fight the wave, it can feel bigger. If you ride it, it passes sooner.

One helpful trick is to name what is happening without insulting yourself. Instead of "I'm freaking out," you can think, "My alarm is loud right now." That small change matters. It turns the moment from a shame story into a body story.

Another helpful step is to slow your breathing on purpose. When you breathe slower, you send a message to your brain: "We are not in an emergency." The message does not fix everything instantly, but it lowers the volume. It gives your thinking mind a chance to return.

It also helps to give your body something steady to do. Press your feet into the floor. Feel your toes inside your shoes. Notice one thing you can see, one thing you can hear, and one thing you can touch. These are small anchors. They pull you back into the present.

Some kids and teens try to win by pretending they feel nothing. That usually backfires. A stronger move is to feel the feeling and still choose your next step. Courage is not the absence of panic. Courage is action with panic in the passenger seat, not the driver's seat.

If your body panics often, that does not mean you are broken. It means your alarm is sensitive. Sensitive alarms can be trained. Training looks like gentle practice, good sleep, movement, and learning what calms you down.

A trusted adult can help too. Not by saying "Don't be nervous," but by being steady with you. Steadiness is contagious. When someone calm stays near you, your nervous system learns calm faster.

Confidence in a judgmental world is not only a thought. It is also a skill in your body. When you learn to calm the alarm, you do not become fearless. You become free enough to do what matters.

CHAPTER 7 - Brave Boundaries

A boundary is not a wall that keeps everyone out. A boundary is a line that keeps you safe and keeps relationships clear. It is how you protect your time, your body, your privacy, and your heart.

In a judgmental world, boundaries matter because pressure is everywhere. Pressure can sound friendly: "Come on, everyone is doing it." Pressure can sound like a joke: "Don't be so sensitive." Pressure can sound like a dare: "If you don't do it, you're scared."

Boundaries are how you stay yourself when the crowd is loud. They help you remember that belonging should not cost you your dignity.

Some boundaries are about your body. You get to decide who touches you and how. Some are about your space. You get to decide when you need quiet. Some are about your mind. You get to decide what you watch, what you scroll, and what you feed your attention.

A common worry is, "If I set a boundary, people will dislike me." That can happen. But it is also true that some people respect you more when you are clear. And if someone only likes you when you have no boundaries, that is not real friendship. That is control.

Boundaries do not have to be dramatic. They can be calm. You can say no with a steady voice. You can step back without a speech. You can leave a chat without a fight.

It helps to know the difference between discomfort and danger. Discomfort is when something feels awkward but safe, like trying a new sport or speaking to a new classmate. Danger is when someone is pressuring you to hide, break rules, or do something that could harm you or someone else. Boundaries become stronger when you treat danger as a stop sign.

Peer pressure works best when it makes you hurry. A brave boundary slows the moment down. "I'm going to think." "I'm not doing that." "I'm leaving now." Short sentences are powerful because they are hard to argue with.

Online boundaries matter too. Your phone can be a tool, but it can also be a trap. If a group chat becomes mean, you are allowed to mute it, leave it, or show it to an adult. You are not required to stay in a place that harms your mind.

A strong boundary also includes kindness. Kindness does not mean you say yes. Kindness means you keep your voice respectful while you protect yourself. You can be firm without being cruel.

Sometimes boundaries need backup. If a person keeps pushing, your job is not to handle it alone. Tell a trusted adult. Bring it into the light. A healthy boundary is not secrecy; it is clarity.

Every time you set a boundary, you practice self-respect. Self-respect is the quiet engine under confidence. It says, "I matter enough to protect my life." That belief makes you harder to manipulate and easier to trust.

Boundaries do not make you difficult. Boundaries make you clear. And clarity is one of the strongest forms of confidence.

CHAPTER 8 - Mean Words and Safe Help

Words can build you, and words can bruise you. In a judgmental world, some people use words like rocks. They throw them to look powerful or to hide their own insecurity.

Mean words do not always come from strangers. Sometimes they come from classmates, teammates, even friends. That makes it extra confusing, because you may want to belong and also want to feel safe.

When someone is unkind, your brain may rush to a painful idea: "Something must be wrong with me." But another explanation is often true: something is wrong with the way that person is choosing to act.

There is a difference between feedback and cruelty. Feedback is meant to help you improve. Cruelty is meant to shrink you. Cruelty does not deserve a polite place in your head.

Confidence does not mean you never feel hurt. It means you do not let hurt decide your worth. Your worth is not voted on by a loud kid, a group chat, or a comment section.

If you are being teased, mocked, or bullied, safety comes first. Safety might mean stepping away, going to a supervised place, staying near supportive peers, and letting adults know. You are not tattling. You are protecting yourself. That is a mature skill.

Some kids try to solve bullying by becoming mean back. That usually spreads the fire. A steadier approach protects your dignity and uses help wisely. You do not have to win an argument to win your life.

Online meanness can feel endless because it follows you. Screens can make cruel people feel brave. If a message is threatening or humiliating, do not carry it alone. Save evidence, block when possible, and involve a trusted adult. Light makes it smaller.

It also helps to remember that groups can get weird. In a crowd, people sometimes laugh at things they do not truly believe, just to fit in. That does not excuse harm, but it explains why unkindness can spread. Your job is to stay human while you protect yourself.

If you are a bystander—someone watching unkindness happen—you have power too. You might not be able to stop everything, but you can refuse to join in. You can check on the person who was targeted. You can tell an adult. Small brave choices change the temperature of a room.

After a mean moment, your mind may replay it again and again. That replay can feel like a trap. A helpful move is to return to the Reporter voice: "This happened. It hurt." Then add a truth: "It is not the full story of me."

Confidence grows when you build a safe circle. A safe circle includes at least one adult and at least one peer who treats you with respect. When your circle is real, you do not have to chase approval from people who harm you.

The goal is not to become hard. The goal is to become steady. Steady people can feel pain and still keep their dignity.

They can ask for help and still be strong. In a judgmental world, that steadiness is a superpower.

CHAPTER 9 - The Courage to Be a Beginner

Being a beginner is brave. It does not feel brave, because beginners look clumsy. Beginners make mistakes in public. Beginners ask simple questions. Beginners don't know the secret shortcuts yet.

A judgmental world tries to make beginners feel embarrassed. It whispers, "You should already be good." It laughs when someone trips over a new skill. But that whisper is not truth. It is pressure pretending to be wisdom.

Every strong person you admire was a beginner first. No one starts as a champion. No one starts as a great writer. No one starts as a calm leader. They become those things by being a beginner longer than other people were willing to.

The hardest part of being a beginner is not the skill. It is the feeling. Embarrassment is a loud feeling. It tries to push you back into hiding. But embarrassment is not danger. It is just a social sting.

Confidence grows when you can handle the sting without quitting. You can say, "This feels awkward," and still keep practicing. You can blush and still take the next step. That is real strength.

One helpful idea is to shrink the stage. If starting feels too public, begin in a smaller setting. Practice at home first. Practice with one trusted friend. Practice where mistakes feel safe. Then slowly move into bigger spaces. Courage is built in levels, not in one giant leap.

Another helpful idea is to measure progress correctly. Beginners often compare their first week to someone else's tenth year. That is not fair to your brain. Compare yourself to yesterday instead. Small improvements are still improvements. They are the bricks of skill.

It also helps to choose a "practice identity." Instead of "I have to prove I'm talented," your practice identity says, "I am a learner." Learners are allowed to be slow. Learners are allowed to repeat things. Learners are allowed to need help.

Perfectionism is the enemy of beginner courage. Perfectionism says, "If you can't do it perfectly, don't do it at all." That rule steals your future. The real rule is kinder: "Do it badly at first. Then do it better."

People might still judge. Some will. But you do not have to give them the steering wheel. Their opinion is a sound outside your house. Your choices are inside your house. You can hear the sound and still keep building your life.

There is also a quiet reward for beginners: pride. Not pride that shouts, but pride that warms you. It comes from doing something hard on purpose. It comes from showing up again.

When you practice being a beginner, you practice a future skill too: starting over. Life will ask you to start over many times—new schools, new teams, new friendships, new responsibilities. A confident person is not the person who never starts over. A confident person is the person who knows they can.

Your courage as a beginner is not small. It is the doorway to everything you will learn next.

CHAPTER 10 - Your Inner Coach

Everyone has a voice inside their head. It comments while you live your life. Sometimes it is helpful. Sometimes it is harsh.

A harsh inner voice can sound like a bully. It calls you names. It makes everything dramatic. It turns one mistake into a disaster: "You always mess up." "Everyone thinks you're weird." "You're not good enough."

That voice often borrows lines from the outside world— things people said, things you heard, things you feared. But just because a thought is loud does not mean it is true.

A healthier inner voice is not fake positivity. It is honest and steady. It sees the problem and still respects you. It sounds more like a coach: "That didn't go the way you wanted. Let's learn and try again."

You can build an inner coach on purpose. The first step is noticing the difference between criticism and guidance. Criticism attacks your identity. Guidance points to an action. "You're hopeless" is criticism. "Study this part again" is guidance.

The next step is choosing language that keeps your dignity. Dignity does not mean you never correct yourself. It means you correct yourself without destroying yourself.

A simple question can help: "Would I say this to a younger kid I care about?" If the answer is no, the sentence does not deserve to live in your head as your daily voice. You can rewrite it into something true and usable.

Rewriting does not mean pretending everything is fine. It means turning the volume down on shame and turning the volume up on learning. For example, "I'm terrible at math" becomes "This chapter is hard, so I will practice the type of problem I missed."

Your inner coach also remembers your wins. Not only trophies—wins like trying again, apologizing, asking for help, or staying kind when you were upset. When you only track mistakes, your brain thinks you are unsafe. When you track growth, your brain relaxes.

If you want confidence, treat your attention like a flashlight. A flashlight can point at everything wrong, or it can also point at what is working. A balanced mind does both. It corrects and it encourages.

Sometimes the harsh voice gets louder when you are tired, hungry, overstimulated, or lonely. That is not your personality. That is your nervous system asking for care. Food, water, sleep, movement, and connection are not rewards. They are maintenance for your mind.

You do not have to become perfect to become confident. You only need to become trustworthy to yourself. Trust grows when your inner voice is fair. Fair does not mean easy. Fair means truthful, kind, and focused on the next step.

In a judgmental world, your inner coach is a private place of safety you carry everywhere. When you speak to yourself with respect, you become harder to break and easier to grow.

CHAPTER 11 - The Comparison Trap

Comparison is one of the brain's oldest habits. It helps people learn quickly: watching how others run, draw, solve problems, or make friends. But in a judgmental world, comparison can turn into a trap. Instead of learning, it starts ranking. And ranking makes confidence feel fragile.

The trap works like this: you look at someone else's highlight and treat it like their whole life. You see the grade, the trophy, the popular group, the perfect outfit, the calm smile. You do not see the practice, the nerves, the help they received, the mistakes they made, or the parts they hide.

Even in real life, you only see a slice of the story. And online, you often see the most polished slice. When your brain compares your ordinary day to someone else's edited moment, you end up feeling behind—even if you are growing.

Comparison can pull in two directions. Upward comparison says, "They are better than me," and it can shrink you. Downward comparison says, "At least I'm better than them," and it can harden you. Neither direction makes you steady. Steady confidence does not need to stand on someone else's back.

A healthier move is to shift from ranking to learning. When you notice someone doing well, their success can become information instead of a threat. It becomes a reminder that skills can be built, and that effort can show up as results over time.

Learning from others does not require copying them. It requires noticing what is useful. One person's method might fit your brain. Another person's method might not. Confidence grows when you choose what helps and leave the rest behind.

Another strong move is to compare in the right lane. The fairest comparison is not you versus someone else's life. The fairest comparison is you today versus you before. That kind of comparison does not make you small. It makes you clear. It shows you that you are moving.

Jealousy often appears in the comparison trap. Jealousy is not proof that you are a bad person. Jealousy is often a signal that something matters to you. It points toward a wish: more attention, more skill, more freedom, more belonging, more respect.

When jealousy is treated like a signal, it can become fuel. Instead of turning into bitterness, it can turn into a plan. A plan can be small and quiet: practice a little more, ask for help, try again, join a new group, take one brave step.

It also helps to remember that life is not one scoreboard. There are many kinds of strength. Some people are fast. Some people are kind under pressure. Some people are creative. Some people are steady. A judgmental world often rewards the loudest strengths, but your future needs the deeper ones too.

Confidence becomes sturdier when you stop treating other people's wins as your losses. Someone else doing well does not erase your chance to grow. There is room for many people to improve, shine, and belong at the same time.

If comparison keeps grabbing your attention, it may help to choose what you feed your mind. The brain becomes what it watches. If your feed makes you feel smaller, it is not a neutral tool—it is a shaping tool. When you choose kinder influences, your confidence has better soil.

In the end, comparison is only helpful when it points you toward learning and hope. If it points you toward shame, it is not truth. It is a trap. You do not have to live inside it. You can step out, breathe, and return to your own path.

CHAPTER 12 - When Worth Feels Like a Score

In school and sports and activities, numbers show up everywhere. Grades, rankings, time trials, scores, levels, likes. Numbers can be useful. They can measure something real. But numbers are not a full person.

A judgmental world often whispers the same message in different forms: "Your value is your result." That message sounds serious, but it is not true. A result is a snapshot. You are a whole movie.

A test score tells you how you performed on one day, with one set of questions, under one set of conditions. It does not tell the full story of your effort. It does not measure your kindness. It does not measure your courage. It does not measure your future.

When people treat scores like identity, fear grows. Fear tries to protect you by pushing you toward perfection. Perfection sounds like safety, but it often creates more pressure. It makes one mistake feel like a collapse.

A steadier way to live with evaluation is to separate two things: results and worth. Results can change. Worth does not. Your worth is the fact that you are a human being. It is not something you earn with a grade.

Confidence under pressure is not pretending you do not care. It is caring without breaking yourself. It is studying with focus, then sleeping, then showing up. It is doing your best without demanding a perfect performance.

A good preparation style is gentle and consistent. Instead of cramming and panicking, steady practice teaches your brain to trust you. When you work in small pieces, your mind stays clearer and your confidence grows quietly.

During a test or performance, the loudest problem is often your thoughts, not the questions. If the mind starts shouting, the body reacts. Breathing tightens. Hands get tense. Time feels faster. In that moment, a calm rhythm matters more than a heroic burst. Calm is how you access what you already know.

After a result arrives, the inner voice matters again. A harsh voice turns a number into an insult. A coach voice turns a number into information. Information can be used. Insults can't.

It helps to treat results like a map, not a judge. A map shows where you are and where you can go next. A judge only announces punishment. Learning needs a map, not a courtroom.

Sometimes adults add pressure without meaning to. They worry about your future, so they push. But pressure without connection does not build confidence. It builds fear. Confidence grows best when expectations come with support: clear plans, realistic pacing, and respect for your limits.

If you feel stuck, asking for help is not weakness. It is strategy. It is maturity. A tutor, a teacher, a coach, or a parent can help you find what you missed, not what you are.

There will be days when you do not meet your goal. That can hurt. But missing a goal is not the same as being a failure. It is simply a signal that a plan needs adjusting.

In a judgmental world, it is tempting to chase only applause. But applause fades fast. Skills last longer. When you focus on building skill and character, scores become one part of the story—not the whole story.

Your life is bigger than a report card. Your future is bigger than one season. When you remember that, you can work hard with a lighter heart. And that lighter heart makes you stronger.

CHAPTER 13 - Belonging Without Disappearing

Most people want the same thing, even if they act like they don't: to belong. Belonging feels like a warm place in a cold world. It says, "I am not alone."

In a judgmental world, belonging can get confusing. Sometimes kids and teens try to buy belonging with silence. They laugh at jokes they don't like. They agree when they don't agree. They hide what they love. They shrink their real self to fit into a shape that gets approval.

That kind of belonging is not a home. It is a mask. And wearing a mask for too long is exhausting. Confidence fades when you disappear to be accepted.

Real belonging is different. Real belonging does not require you to become someone else. It allows you to be yourself and still be treated with respect. Respect is the basic floor of a healthy friendship.

Some friendships are loud and fun, but not safe. Some are quiet, but deeply loyal. A good friend is not perfect. A good friend is consistent. They do not punish you for having feelings. They do not use your secrets as weapons. They do not make you prove your worth every day.

Sometimes the most painful social moments are about exclusion. A group might leave you out, whisper, or make plans without you. That hurts for a real reason: humans are wired for connection. Feeling hurt does not mean you are weak. It means you are human.

Exclusion can also trick you into chasing the wrong people. If you run after every door that closes, you may miss the doors that are open. Confidence grows when you stop begging for a seat at a table that keeps pushing you away.

Finding your people often happens through shared interests and shared values. Clubs, sports, music, art, science, volunteering, games, books—these are not just activities. They are places where your natural self has something to do, so friendship can grow without forcing it.

Belonging also grows through small acts of courage. Courage can be as simple as saying hello, sitting near kind people, joining a conversation, or inviting someone to work together. Small brave choices build social strength the way small workouts build muscles.

At the same time, healthy belonging includes boundaries. You can be friendly and still say no. You can care about people and still leave a situation that feels mean. When you respect yourself, you choose relationships that respect you back.

Sometimes friendships change. A friend can drift. A group can split. You can outgrow a circle. That can feel like loss. And it is okay to feel sad about it. But change does not mean you are unlovable. It means life is moving.

The most reliable way to build belonging is to practice being the kind of friend you hope to have. Kindness, honesty, and steadiness attract the same qualities over time. You cannot control who likes you, but you can control what kind of person you become.

In a judgmental world, belonging is not about winning popularity. It is about finding safety, respect, and real connection. When you do not disappear to be accepted, you grow a stronger kind of confidence—the kind that stays with you wherever you go.

CHAPTER 14 - Life Online, Real Life You

The internet can be amazing. It can teach you, connect you, entertain you, and help you find people who share your interests. But it can also become a loud judgment machine. It can make you feel watched, compared, and scored.

Online, many things are turned into numbers: views, likes, followers, streaks. Those numbers can feel like a vote on who matters. But they are not a vote. They are a measurement of attention, not worth.

The online world is also full of highlights. People post the best angles, the funniest moments, the biggest wins. The hard parts are often edited out. When you forget that, you may start thinking everyone else is living an easier life than you are.

Confidence online begins with remembering something simple: the screen is not the whole world. It is one window. And windows can distort. The closer you press your face to the glass, the harder it is to see the rest of your life.

A steady online life usually has one clear rule: the phone is a tool, not a boss. When the phone becomes the boss, your mood starts being managed by notifications. That is not freedom. That is being pulled.

One of the healthiest shifts is moving from consuming to creating. Consuming means watching and scrolling until your brain feels full and tired. Creating means making something: a story, a drawing, a song, a model, a video with care, a message that helps someone. Creating builds identity. Endless consuming often drains it.

Another steady habit is choosing your inputs. Feeds are not neutral. They shape what your brain believes is normal. If your feed makes you feel worse about your body, your face, your life, or your pace, it is not "just entertainment." It is training your attention to judge you. You deserve better training.

Comments can be tricky. Some comments are thoughtful. Some are careless. Some are cruel. A cruel comment often says more about the writer than about you. You do not have to hold every stranger's opinion in your hands like it is precious.

If online cruelty becomes bullying, secrecy makes it heavier. Saving messages, blocking when possible, and involving a trusted adult is not overreacting. It is protecting your mind. You deserve support when someone tries to harm you.

Privacy is part of confidence too. A confident person does not need to share everything to feel real. Keeping personal information safe is not paranoia; it is wisdom. You can be open-hearted without being unprotected.

The goal online is not to become famous. The goal is to stay human. Human means you rest. Human means you go outside. Human means you talk to real people and feel real weather. Human means your life does not shrink into a rectangle.

When you use the internet with intention, it can be a powerful ally. When you use it without intention, it can become a mirror that lies. Confidence grows when you choose the ally and walk away from the lying mirror.

CHAPTER 15 - A Compass Inside

Confidence is not only a feeling. It is also a direction. When you know what matters to you, you move with more steadiness—even when people judge.

A judgmental world tries to make you chase whatever is popular. It offers a simple deal: "Be what we like, and we will approve of you." But approval changes fast. The crowd can clap today and criticize tomorrow. A life built only on applause is a life that shakes in every wind.

A steadier life is guided by something inside: values. Values are the qualities you want to live by, even when nobody is watching. They are not a list you memorize. They are a kind of compass that points you toward your best self.

Some kids value kindness. Some value courage. Some value creativity. Some value fairness. Some value curiosity. Many people value more than one thing. Values can grow as you grow. The important part is that your values belong to you, not to the loudest voices around you.

When you live by values, you can still care what people think, but you are not controlled by it. You can hear criticism and still choose your next step. You can feel nervous and still do what you believe is right.

Purpose is often misunderstood. Purpose is not always one giant mission. For many people, purpose is built from small choices repeated over time. It is the habit of aiming your life toward something meaningful, even in ordinary days.

A purpose-shaped life asks a simple question underneath everything: "What kind of person am I practicing being?" You practice being a person by what you do when you are tired, when you are tempted, when you are scared, and when you are praised.

Goals can help, but goals are not the same as values. A goal is an outcome. A value is a way of living. Outcomes can be blocked by luck, timing, or other people. A way of living is yours to choose every day.

That is why process goals are powerful. A process goal is something you can do: practice, read, train, ask questions, show up, rest, apologize, try again. When you build strong processes, outcomes often improve as a side effect.

A compass also helps you say no. When you know what matters, you can choose what does not fit. You can step away from drama. You can decline pressure. You can protect your time. Saying no becomes less scary when you have a yes you are protecting.

Even with a compass, you will get lost sometimes. Everyone does. Getting lost does not mean you are broken. It means you are human in a complicated world. The skill is returning—returning to values, returning to the inner coach, returning to the next small step.

Confidence grows when you live with this quiet promise: "I will not abandon myself." You can make mistakes and still respect yourself. You can struggle and still keep going. That promise turns confidence into something you can rely on.

A judgmental world will keep making noise. Your compass helps you walk anyway. When you move in the direction of what matters, your life becomes more than a performance. It becomes a journey with meaning, and you become the kind of person who can carry that meaning forward.

CHAPTER 16 - Words That Sting

Sometimes a single sentence can land like a slap. A joke that isn't funny. A comment about your body. A teacher's sharp tone. A friend's eye roll. In a judgmental world, words can feel like they decide who you are.

The truth is simpler and kinder: words are not rulers. They are signals. Some signals are accurate, some are noisy, and some are meant to hurt. Your job is not to collect every signal. Your job is to learn which ones deserve space in your mind.

There is a difference between feedback and judgment. Feedback points to a specific behavior and tries to help you improve. Judgment labels you as a person: "You're lazy," "You're weird," "You're a loser." Labels feel powerful because they are short. But short does not mean true.

When a comment hits hard, your brain reacts fast. Social pain can light up the body like physical pain. That is why teasing can feel bigger than it looks. Your reaction is not "too much." It is your nervous system doing its job.

Still, you do not have to obey the reaction. You can learn to pause between the sting and your next move. That pause is where confidence lives. It is the small gap where you choose: "Will I carry this, or will I set it down?"

A steady way to sort comments is to run them through three quiet filters. First: is it true? Second: is it useful? Third: is it kind or at least respectful? A comment that fails all three filters is not guidance. It is noise. You can let noise pass without fighting it.

Sometimes the hardest comments are the ones that are partly true. Maybe you did forget something. Maybe you did speak too loudly. Even then, the helpful part is the behavior, not the insult. You can take the useful piece and leave the cruelty behind.

When criticism comes from someone who is trying to help—like a teacher, coach, or caregiver—it can still feel uncomfortable. Confidence does not mean you love criticism. It means you can use it without shrinking. A confident learner turns feedback into a next step, not a life sentence.

Teasing and bullying are different. Teasing can be clumsy and occasional. Bullying repeats and aims to harm. If someone keeps targeting you, making you afraid, or turning others against you, you do not need to handle it alone. Getting adult support is not tattling. It is safety.

A judgmental world often admires the kid who "doesn't care." But real strength is not pretending. Real strength is protection. Protection can look like walking away, blocking online, sitting near kinder people, or saying one calm sentence and ending the conversation.

Your voice matters, but it does not need to be dramatic to be strong. A steady voice is often the most powerful. When you speak with calm boundaries, you teach people how to treat you. And you teach yourself that you are worth protecting.

Some words will still get through. That is normal. Confidence is not a perfect shield. When you feel hurt, the goal is not to bully yourself for being sensitive. The goal is to care for the hurt part and return to your center.

Your center is the place inside that remembers: your worth is not up for voting. You can learn, grow, and improve, but you do not have to prove you deserve respect. Respect is the starting point. And the most important respect is the one you practice toward yourself.

In a judgmental world, you will hear many opinions. You get to choose which ones become lessons, and which ones become dust.

CHAPTER 17 - The Bounce-Back Skill

People often think confident kids never mess up. But that is not how confidence works. Confidence is not a life with no falls. Confidence is the skill of standing up again without hating yourself.

Mistakes are part of learning in the same way bumps are part of growing taller. They are uncomfortable, but they mean something is changing. Your brain is built to learn from errors. It adjusts its map when something does not work. That is why practice feels awkward before it feels smooth.

A judgmental world turns mistakes into shame. Shame says, "Something is wrong with me." But a mistake is usually much smaller than that. A mistake says, "Something I tried didn't work yet." Yet is a powerful word. It keeps the door open.

After a mistake, many kids feel an urge to hide. Hiding feels safe for a moment, but it often makes the problem heavier. A steadier path is to face what happened with clear eyes and a kind inner voice. Kind does not mean fake. Kind means useful and fair.

Bounce-back begins with a reset. A reset can be as small as a slow breath, loosening your shoulders, and taking one sip of water. Your body needs a signal that you are not in danger. When the body calms, the mind can think again.

Then comes the simple truth: name what happened without adding insults. "I forgot my homework" is a fact. "I'm stupid" is a story. Facts help you solve problems. Stories like that only hurt you.

Next comes repair. Repair is one of the most confident things a person can do. Repair can mean apologizing, replacing what you broke, making up a missed assignment, or practicing a skill you avoided. Repair says, "I take responsibility, and I believe I can improve."

Sometimes you cannot fully fix the result. A game stays lost. A grade stays on the paper. But you can still fix the direction. Direction is what matters most in the long run. The future belongs to people who adjust and continue.

A helpful way to think is: every mistake gives you data. Data is not a punishment. Data is a message. The message might be "start earlier," "ask for help," "slow down," or "practice the basics." When you treat mistakes as data, you become a learner instead of a judge.

Another part of bounce-back is how you talk to yourself when nobody else is listening. A harsh inner voice does not make you stronger. It makes you scared, and fear makes learning harder. A coach voice can be firm and still respectful. It pushes you forward without crushing you.

Some kids worry that being kind to themselves will make them lazy. It does not. Self-respect creates courage. Courage creates effort. Effort creates growth. The strongest people are not the ones who shout at themselves; they are the ones who return to the work.

There will be days when you feel embarrassed. That feeling can be heavy, but it is not permanent. Embarrassment fades when you stop replaying the scene like a punishment. It fades faster when you take one small brave action that moves you forward.

Bounce-back is not a trick you learn once. It is a habit you practice. Every time you recover from a mistake, you build a stronger nervous system and a steadier heart. You become the kind of person who can handle real life—because real life is full of second chances.

CHAPTER 18 - Brave in Small Steps

Bravery is often misunderstood. Many people picture bravery as loud confidence: no fear, no shaking, no doubt. But real bravery is quieter. Bravery is feeling fear and still moving toward what matters.

Fear is not your enemy. Fear is your body's alarm system. It tries to protect you. The problem is that alarms can be too sensitive. A smoke alarm can beep when toast burns, even though the house is not on fire. In the same way, your body can panic during a presentation, even though you are safe.

A judgmental world sometimes tells kids to "toughen up" by ignoring fear. That rarely works. A steadier skill is to listen to fear, then decide. Some fear is a real warning: danger, violence, unsafe people. That fear should be respected. Some fear is discomfort: trying something new, being seen, making a mistake in public. That fear can be trained.

Training bravery works like training muscles. You do not lift the heaviest weight on the first day. You start with a weight you can handle, and you repeat. Over time, your strength grows. Bravery grows the same way: with small steps that are repeated.

For one kid, a small brave step might be raising a hand in class. For another, it might be joining a new group. For another, it might be telling a friend, "That joke hurts." The step does not have to look impressive to others. It only has to be real for you.

Small bravery is powerful because it teaches your brain a new lesson: "I can feel nervous and still do the thing." That lesson changes your future. It makes school, friendships, sports, and new places less scary over time.

Bravery also includes asking for help. Some kids think help is only for people who are failing. That is not true. Help is for people who are building something. Athletes have coaches. Musicians have teachers. Strong people use support on purpose.

Sometimes bravery is not about doing more. Sometimes it is about stopping. Stopping a mean conversation. Stopping a risky plan. Stopping a habit that hurts you. It takes courage to step away from a crowd when the crowd is going in the wrong direction.

Bravery can also be protective, especially when you see someone else being treated badly. Protective bravery does not mean starting a fight. It means choosing safe action: getting an adult, moving closer to supportive people, inviting the person to walk with you, or refusing to laugh at cruelty.

A judgmental world loves quick results. Bravery often works slowly. You might take a brave step and still feel shaky. That does not mean it failed. It means your nervous system is learning. Learning takes repetition.

Over time, small brave choices stack up. They become your story. Not the story of a kid who was never afraid, but the story of a kid who learned how to live with fear without being ruled by it. That is what confidence looks like when it is real.

CHAPTER 19 - Drama, Gossip, and Pressure

Friendships can feel like sunshine, and they can also feel like weather. Some days are calm. Some days are stormy. In a judgmental world, storms can grow fast—especially when drama and gossip become entertainment.

Drama often starts with a small spark: someone feels left out, someone feels jealous, someone feels misunderstood. Instead of speaking directly, they speak around the person. The story spreads, details change, and suddenly everyone has an opinion.

Gossip feels tempting because it makes you feel included. It offers a quick seat at the table. But gossip is expensive. It costs trust. It teaches people that private stories are not safe around you. And when gossip becomes normal, it turns friendship into a place where everyone is always watching their back.

One of the strongest social skills is to step out of gossip without becoming mean. You do not have to attack anyone. You can simply refuse to carry the story. A calm refusal protects your peace and protects other people too.

Sometimes people gossip because they do not know what to do with their feelings. They turn feelings into stories. You can choose a different path: feelings can be handled with honesty, not with rumor. Honesty does not mean harshness. It means directness and respect.

Peer pressure often arrives wearing a friendly face. It sounds like, "Come on, everyone is doing it." Or, "If you were really my friend, you would." Pressure tries to trade your values for approval.

That is where your inner compass matters. When you know what you stand for, you do not need to argue for hours. You can choose a simple, steady answer and protect your future self. A short no, said with calm, is often stronger than a long explanation.

Not every friendship deserves full access to you. Some kids are fun but reckless. Some are popular but cruel. Some are kind but quiet. The quality of a friendship is not decided by how many people notice it. It is decided by how safe you feel inside it.

A useful clue is how you feel after spending time with someone. Do you feel lighter or smaller? Do you feel respected or tested? Do you feel free to be yourself or forced to perform? Your body often tells the truth before your brain wants to admit it.

When conflict happens, the goal is not to "win." The goal is to protect respect. Some problems can be repaired with honest conversation and a change in behavior. But if someone keeps crossing your boundaries, stepping back is not betrayal. It is self-respect.

If a group turns unkind, you may feel afraid to leave because you worry you will be alone. But staying in a cruel circle often makes you lonelier on the inside. A smaller, kinder friendship can be healthier than a large group that makes you anxious.

Adults sometimes misunderstand social pain because it does not leave bruises. But it is real. If you are being targeted, threatened, or bullied, involve a trusted adult. Strong people do not handle harmful situations alone. They build a team.

Drama feeds on attention. Confidence starves drama by refusing to treat it as entertainment. When you choose honesty, boundaries, and kindness, your social world becomes steadier. And steadiness is a kind of freedom.

CHAPTER 20 - Your Confidence Routine

Some people wait for confidence to "arrive," like a gift that shows up one day. But confidence is more like a routine. It grows when you practice it the way you practice brushing your teeth or tying your shoes.

A judgmental world tries to make confidence depend on other people's reactions. If they clap, you feel good. If they judge, you feel small. That is an exhausting way to live, because you cannot control the crowd.

A steadier confidence is built from things you can control. It rests on three strong legs: caring for your body, guiding your mind, and living with direction. When those three are steady, your confidence becomes less fragile.

Caring for your body sounds simple, but it is powerful. Sleep helps your brain handle stress. Movement helps emotions move through instead of getting stuck. Food and water help your mood stay more even. You do not need a perfect health plan. You need basic care that you repeat.

Guiding your mind means choosing what voice leads you. The judgmental voice is loud, dramatic, and cruel. The coach voice is steady, honest, and respectful. It tells the truth without attacking you. When you practice a coach voice, you become safer inside your own head.

Guiding your mind also includes what you feed it. The brain becomes familiar with what it sees every day. If your media makes you feel smaller, it trains you to judge yourself. When you choose kinder influences—books, friends, videos, music, mentors—your confidence has better soil.

Living with direction means remembering your values and choosing small actions that match them. Direction does not require a huge plan. It can be one small promise you keep: practicing, reading, helping, resting, trying again. Small promises kept over time build a strong identity.

A good routine also includes recovery. No one is confident every hour of every day. Some days you will feel shaky, disappointed, or tired. Recovery means you do not panic about those days. You treat them like weather: real, but temporary.

When you have a hard day, the most helpful move is often the smallest one: return to basics. Drink water. Eat something steady. Sleep. Talk to a trusted adult. Take a walk. These steps may look ordinary, but ordinary steps are what rebuild a life.

As you grow, your confidence routine will change. That is normal. Your needs will change, and your challenges will change. But the deeper rule stays: you are allowed to be a work in progress. You can be learning and still respect yourself.

In a judgmental world, becoming your best self is not about being perfect. It is about being real, steady, and brave enough to keep going. When you practice your routine, you do not just gain confidence. You gain a way of living that can carry you through school, friendships, and the many new chapters ahead.

CHAPTER 21 - The Comparison Trap

Comparison is one of the fastest habits in the human brain. You walk into a room and your mind starts measuring: who is taller, who is louder, who looks confident, who seems liked. It happens before you even decide to do it.

This habit is not proof that you are shallow. It is the brain trying to find your place in a group so you can feel safe. Long ago, belonging helped people survive. Your brain still remembers that old rule, even when you are just trying to enjoy school or a hobby.

The problem begins when comparison turns into a verdict. A verdict sounds like, "They are better, so I am worse." It makes the world feel like a scoreboard where only one person can win. That is not how real growth works.

In real life, you can admire someone and still respect yourself. Their strength does not steal your chances. Someone else's talent is information, not a weapon. It can show you what is possible without saying anything bad about you.

A judgmental world encourages comparison because it is easy to control people who feel small. If you are always trying to prove you are enough, you have less energy to learn, to play, and to become yourself.

Social media makes the comparison trap deeper. Most people post their best moments, not their hardest ones. You see a highlight reel and your brain compares it to your behind-the-scenes life. That is not a fair match.

Confidence grows when you change what you compare. Instead of comparing yourself to someone else's whole life, compare yourself to your own progress. Progress can be quiet: one new word learned, one brave question asked, one calmer reaction.

It also helps to notice what comparison is trying to protect. Sometimes you compare because you fear being rejected. Sometimes you compare because you want to be good at something you care about. Those feelings are normal. They are not enemies.

When comparison appears, you can speak to it like a wise older friend. You can say, "I see what you are doing. You want me to be safe. But making me smaller will not make me safer." That sentence can interrupt the spiral.

Another steady move is to return to your own lane. Your lane is your practice, your effort, your values, and your rhythm. Your lane does not have to look like anyone else's. The goal is not to be the same. The goal is to be real.

Sometimes comparison points to a useful wish. If you feel jealous, your jealousy may be pointing at something you want to learn or try. Jealousy is uncomfortable, but it can be a signpost. You can turn it into a plan instead of a punishment.

There will also be days when comparison hurts more than usual. Those days often happen when you are tired, hungry, stressed, or lonely. On those days, confidence begins with care. Your brain judges more harshly when your body is running low.

A strong, kind rule is this: you are allowed to be a beginner. You are allowed to be in the middle. You are allowed to take time. No one else's timeline gets to be the clock that decides your worth.

In a judgmental world, comparison tries to shrink you. Your job is not to win every comparison. Your job is to keep growing in your own direction. When you do that, confidence becomes something you build, not something you chase.

CHAPTER 22 - Perfectionism vs. Excellence

In a judgmental world, perfectionism can look like a shield. If you do everything perfectly, nobody can criticize you—right? That is what perfectionism promises. But perfectionism is a promise it cannot keep.

Perfectionism does not actually make life safer. It makes life narrower. It tells you, "Do not try unless you can be the best." It turns learning into fear, and it turns mistakes into shame. Over time, it can steal your curiosity.

Excellence is different. Excellence means you care and you work hard, but you also stay human. Excellence leaves room for practice, rest, and improvement. Excellence asks, "What can I learn next?" not "How can I never be wrong?"

One way to tell them apart is to notice your body. Perfectionism often feels tight: tight chest, tight stomach, tight thoughts. Excellence can feel focused, but it still lets you breathe. It is serious without being cruel.

Perfectionism loves all-or-nothing thinking. It says, "If I can't do it perfectly, it's a disaster." But real progress is built from imperfect days stacked together. A musician does not become skilled by playing one perfect song. They become skilled by practicing many messy songs.

A helpful idea is to think in drafts. Your first attempt is a draft. Your second attempt is a better draft. Even grown-ups use drafts: writers, engineers, athletes, scientists. Drafts are not embarrassing. Drafts are how things are made.

This matters a lot in school. Tests and grades are important, but they are not your identity. A grade is one measurement on one day. It can show you what you know and what you still need to practice. It does not get to decide what kind of person you are.

When you feel pressure, bring your attention to what you can control. You can control effort, preparation, asking questions, and returning to practice after a mistake. You cannot control every opinion or every surprise.

If your brain says, "I must be perfect," you can answer, "I will aim for prepared." Prepared is stronger than perfect. Prepared means you showed up. You did the work you could. You used your time wisely. You asked for help when needed.

It is also okay to set a "good enough" line. Good enough does not mean careless. It means realistic. It means finishing a task with your best focus for today, then letting it go so you can sleep, play, and live.

Many kids become perfectionists because they are afraid of disappointing people they love. If you feel that fear, you are not alone. But love is not supposed to feel like a trap. A healthy love helps you grow; it does not demand you never struggle.

When you mess up—and you will, because you are human—practice a repair mindset. Repair mindset says, "What is the next right step?" It does not say, "I am ruined." The next right step might be studying differently, asking a teacher for feedback, or simply trying again tomorrow.

Perfectionism makes you smaller. Excellence makes you steadier. The goal is not to lower your standards. The goal is to raise your support: better habits, kinder self-talk, and a clearer plan.

In a judgmental world, it takes courage to be imperfect on purpose. But that courage is exactly how you become strong. Confidence grows when you keep going, even when the work is not flawless.

CHAPTER 23 - Confidence in Your Voice

Many kids think confidence means being the loudest person in the room. That is not true. Confidence is not volume. Confidence is clarity. It is knowing what you mean and saying it with respect.

In a judgmental world, speaking up can feel risky. You might worry that your question sounds "dumb," or that your opinion will be laughed at, or that a boundary will make people mad. Those worries are common, especially when you care about belonging.

But your voice is one of your strongest tools. It helps you learn, protects your boundaries, and builds healthier relationships. When you do not use your voice, other people's choices can decide your life for you.

Confidence in your voice does not mean you win every conversation. It means you show up honestly. Sometimes honesty is a question. Sometimes it is a request. Sometimes it is a calm no.

A strong voice often begins with one simple habit: slowing down. When you rush, words get tangled. When you slow down, you can choose your sentence. A calm pause can make you sound more certain, even if you feel nervous.

Another helpful habit is to separate facts from attacks. You can describe what happened without insulting anyone. For example: "You took my pencil without asking." That is a fact. It is easier to solve facts than to fight insults.

When you need to set a boundary, a clear structure can help. You can name what happened, name how it affected you, and name what you need next. This is not a magic script. It is just a way to keep your message steady.

Confidence also includes asking for help. Asking for help is not weakness. It is wisdom. A student who asks questions is not annoying; they are building their brain. A kid who asks for support is not "too sensitive;" they are practicing safety.

Sometimes you will speak kindly and someone will still react badly. That does not mean you did something wrong. It may mean the other person is not ready to hear you. You can still hold your boundary and step toward safer people.

There are also moments when your voice should bring in an adult. If there is bullying, threats, or anything that makes you feel unsafe, you do not need to be the hero alone. Getting help is a form of courage.

Confidence in your voice grows through small repetitions. Each time you ask a question in class, each time you say, "Please stop," each time you correct a misunderstanding, you teach your nervous system that speaking up can be safe.

Some kids have quieter personalities, and that is okay. A quiet voice can be powerful. You do not need to perform confidence like a show. You only need to practice truth and respect.

Your voice is also the voice you use inside your head. If your inner voice is cruel, it becomes harder to speak up outside. A kinder inner voice gives you a home base. From that home base, you can take social risks without falling apart.

In a judgmental world, your voice is a way of saying, "I exist, and I matter." You can speak with kindness and still be strong. The goal is not to be feared. The goal is to be clear.

CHAPTER 24 - When You Feel Left Out

Feeling left out hurts because humans are built for connection. When you see a group laughing without you, or you hear about a plan you were not invited to, your body can react as if something dangerous is happening. That reaction is real, even if nobody meant to hurt you.

In a judgmental world, it is easy to turn exclusion into a story about your worth. The story might sound like, "They didn't choose me because I'm not good enough." But exclusion does not always mean rejection, and rejection does not always mean you are unworthy.

Sometimes you are left out by accident. Sometimes plans are small. Sometimes people are thoughtless, not cruel. And sometimes, yes, people are unkind on purpose. The first step is to stay close to the facts instead of the worst story.

Facts sound like: "They went to the park after school." "My name wasn't on the group chat." A story sounds like: "Nobody likes me." When you stay with facts, you can choose a smarter next step.

One steady next step is a simple check-in. You can ask a direct, calm question: "Did I miss something?" Or, "Are you keeping the group small today?" These questions give people a chance to clarify instead of letting your brain fill in the blanks.

If the answer shows it was an accident, you can decide what you want. You might join. Or you might decide you prefer something else. Being invited is nice, but being free is also powerful.

If the answer shows unkindness, do not chase people who enjoy shrinking you. Chasing teaches them that your peace is available for them to play with. Confidence means stepping away from the table that serves disrespect.

Being left out can also be a signal that your circle needs to change. Your best friendships will not require you to beg for basic kindness. They will feel safer and steadier.

Sometimes the hardest part is the lonely space after you step away. That space can feel like proof that something is wrong with you. But it is not proof. It is a transition. In transitions, you build new connections.

New connections often begin small: one friendly classmate, one club, one hobby, one neighbor, one cousin, one teammate. You do not need a huge group. You need a few people who treat you with respect.

It also helps to build a friendship with yourself. That does not mean you never need others. It means you can be kind company to your own mind. When you like your own presence, exclusion loses some of its power.

On difficult days, return to your basics: sleep, food, movement, and one trusted adult. Social pain can grow when you carry it alone. It shrinks when you name it to someone safe.

If exclusion turns into bullying—repeating, targeting, threatening—do not handle it silently. Involve adults and ask for a clear safety plan. You deserve protection, not just advice.

In a judgmental world, groups can look like kings and queens. But groups change. Popularity changes. Your worth does not change. The right people will not make you earn a seat by losing yourself.

CHAPTER 25 - Your North Star

Confidence is not only a feeling. It is also a direction. When you know what matters to you, you do not have to be pushed around by every opinion. Your values become a steady guide.

A value is something you believe is important, even when nobody is watching. Values are not the same as popularity. Popularity changes quickly. Values are the deeper part of you that stays.

Think of your values as a North Star. Sailors used stars to navigate when the ocean was dark. The North Star did not tell them every wave, but it helped them keep direction. Your values work the same way when life feels confusing.

In a judgmental world, people will try to hand you a different map. They might say, "Be cool," "Be perfect," "Be tough," "Be quiet," or "Be like me." Some advice can be helpful. But some advice is just pressure.

When you live by pressure, you start performing instead of living. You become a version of yourself that is always scanning the crowd. It is exhausting. A value-based life is calmer because your choices come from inside, not from the room.

Values can be simple. You might care about kindness, curiosity, courage, fairness, creativity, loyalty, faith, or learning. You do not need to choose the "best" value. You need to notice what feels true and strong in you.

Once you know what matters, you can use it to make decisions. When you face a tough choice, you can ask: "Which option matches the person I want to be?" That question is powerful because it protects your future self.

Values also help you handle judgment. If someone mocks you for studying, but learning matters to you, you can keep going. If someone pressures you to join cruelty, but kindness matters to you, you can step away. You may still feel nervous, but your direction stays steady.

A purpose does not have to be huge. Many kids think purpose is a big speech or a perfect plan. But purpose often begins small: helping one person, improving one skill, caring for a pet, making something with your hands, or showing up with a good attitude.

Over time, small purposes connect. They form a life that feels meaningful. Meaning is not about being famous. Meaning is about being useful, honest, and alive in your own way.

Your North Star also includes how you treat yourself. Self-respect is a value. When you practice self-respect, you stop talking to yourself like an enemy. You become your own teammate.

There will be moments when you feel lost. Everyone does. In those moments, return to one value and one next step. One value can guide one action, and one action can guide your day back into shape.

In a judgmental world, confidence can look like a loud performance. But the deepest confidence is quieter. It is the confidence of a kid who knows what matters, keeps learning, and keeps choosing direction over noise.

You do not need to impress everyone. You only need to build a life you can respect. When your North Star is clear, your path becomes brighter—even on cloudy days.

CHAPTER 26 - The Art of Feedback

In a judgmental world, feedback can feel like a spotlight that is too bright. Someone comments on your work, your behavior, or your choices, and your body reacts before your mind has time to sort it out. Your heart might race. Your face might get hot. Your thoughts might jump to one sentence: "I'm not good enough."

But feedback is not one thing. It is a mix of information and emotion. Some feedback is meant to help. Some is careless. Some is just someone else's bad mood spilling onto you. If you treat every comment like a final verdict, you will carry a heavy backpack that was never yours to carry.

A useful way to think about feedback is to imagine you have a filter. The filter does not block everything. It simply separates what is helpful from what is noise. A strong filter lets you learn without letting other people own your confidence.

Helpful feedback usually has two signs: it is specific, and it points to a next step. "Your introduction is clear. Add one example so the reader understands faster." That kind of feedback does not attack you. It talks about the work. It also gives a direction.

Unhelpful feedback often feels vague or cruel. "You're terrible." "That's dumb." "Why are you like this?" Those sentences do not teach. They only sting. When someone uses shame instead of clarity, you are allowed to protect yourself.

Protection can be quiet. It can be a pause. It can be stepping away. It can be choosing not to argue. Not every comment deserves a debate. Sometimes the strongest move is to keep your peace and let the noise pass.

When you receive feedback, try giving yourself a small moment to breathe before you respond. A short pause is not weakness. It is your brain giving itself time to stay smart. Fast reactions are often made by fear. Calm reactions are made by choice.

Then ask one simple question inside your mind: "Is there a useful piece here?" If the answer is yes, keep that piece. If the answer is no, do not force yourself to carry it. Your heart is not a trash can for other people's frustration.

Sometimes feedback is partly useful and partly messy. Maybe the person is right about what happened, but wrong about who you are. For example, you may have forgotten a homework page. That is a real mistake. But it does not mean you are lazy forever. You are a person who forgot one page, and you can fix that.

If you are not sure what someone means, it is okay to ask for clarity. A calm question like "Can you show me what you mean?" turns judgment into information. It also helps you avoid guessing, and guessing is where insecurity grows.

Feedback also feels different depending on who says it. A coach, teacher, or caregiver may speak firmly because they want you to improve. A friend may give feedback because they care about fairness. A stranger online may speak harshly because they feel powerful. Knowing the source helps you choose how much weight to give it.

It is also okay to decide the timing. If you feel flooded, you can say, "I want to hear you, but I need a moment." You can return when your body is calmer. Listening with a calm mind is a skill, not a personality trait.

After you process feedback, do one small thing that proves you are still in charge of your growth. That small thing might be fixing one sentence, practicing one skill, or setting one boundary. Confidence grows when you respond with action instead of collapsing into shame.

In a judgmental world, people may try to use feedback as a weapon. You do not have to accept that game. You can turn feedback back into what it is supposed to be: information that helps you improve, and a reminder that your worth is bigger than one comment.

CHAPTER 27 - Confidence Under Pressure

Pressure is not always the enemy. Sometimes pressure means you care. A test matters to you. A performance matters. A game matters. Your body notices that and sends energy to help you act.

That energy can feel like nerves: shaky hands, fast thoughts, a tight throat. Many kids think those feelings mean, "I am not confident." But often they simply mean, "My body is preparing." Confidence is not a lack of nerves. Confidence is knowing what to do with them.

In a judgmental world, pressure can get louder because it feels like people are watching. You may imagine teachers, classmates, or family members holding a scoreboard in their minds. When that picture appears, your brain may rush into fear: "If I mess up, I will be judged."

Here is a calmer truth: people notice less than you think, and they forget faster than you expect. Most people are busy with their own worries. You do not have to perform a perfect life to belong in the world.

To build confidence under pressure, focus on what you can control. You can control preparation, effort, and your next small step. You cannot control every question on a test, every bounce of a ball, or every opinion. Confidence grows when you place your attention where your power actually is.

A simple routine can help your body feel safer. A routine is like a seatbelt: it does not remove every risk, but it helps you stay steady when the road gets bumpy. Before pressure moments, routines can include a few slow breaths, a sip of water, and a clear first action.

When the moment begins, your job is not to win the whole thing at once. Your job is to start well. A test is one question at a time. A speech is one sentence at a time. A game is one play at a time. Starting well brings your mind back into the present, where you can actually do the work.

If you freeze, treat freezing like a signal, not a disaster. It simply means your nervous system is overloaded. You can reset by making your body slightly calmer: drop your shoulders, press your feet into the floor, and breathe out longer than you breathe in. Long exhales tell your brain, "We are safe enough to continue."

Another strong move is to give yourself process language instead of score language. Score language sounds like, "I must get an A," or "I must not miss." Process language sounds like, "Read carefully," "Show my work," "Listen for the beat," or "Stay on my feet." Process language keeps you in action.

After the pressure moment, do not punish yourself with a replay that only looks for mistakes. Review like a coach: notice one thing that worked and one thing to improve next time. A harsh review makes you afraid of the next chance. A fair review makes you stronger for the next chance.

Some kids carry pressure because they believe love depends on results. If you feel that fear, remember this: healthy love does not demand that you never struggle. Healthy love helps you grow, even when you stumble.

It also helps to remember that your life is bigger than one event. A single test does not decide your future. A single game does not decide your identity. Your future is built by many ordinary days of practice and learning.

In a judgmental world, pressure tries to turn you into a statue: stiff and afraid. But you are not a statue. You are a growing person. When you learn how to breathe, begin, and return to process, pressure becomes something you can carry—without letting it carry you.

CHAPTER 28 - Your Inner Coach

In a judgmental world, people may judge you out loud. But the loudest judge is often the one inside your own mind. That inner voice follows you to school, to practice, and into your bedroom at night. If the inner voice is cruel, confidence has a hard time growing.

Many kids think harsh self-talk will keep them from making mistakes. They believe being tough on themselves will make them improve. But harsh self-talk usually does the opposite. It makes you anxious, and anxious brains learn more slowly. A brain that feels safe can focus. A brain that feels attacked tries to escape.

Your inner voice can be trained. You do not have to accept the first thought that appears. Thoughts are not always facts. They are often guesses, fears, and old messages that got stuck.

A helpful idea is to imagine two characters in your mind. One is the inner critic. The other is the inner coach. The critic shouts, "You always mess up." The coach says, "That was hard. Let's try again with a better plan." Both voices want you to be okay, but only one voice helps you get there.

The goal is not to destroy your critic. The goal is to turn down its volume and upgrade its language. Instead of "I'm stupid," you can train your mind to say, "I don't understand this yet." The word yet is small, but it opens a door.

An inner coach speaks in three ways: truth, kindness, and next steps. Truth means you do not pretend everything is perfect. Kindness means you do not attack yourself. Next steps means you keep moving instead of getting stuck in shame.

Here is what that can sound like. Truth: "I forgot my lines." Kindness: "That happens to humans." Next step: "I will practice ten minutes tonight and ask my teacher for one tip." Notice how this kind of self-talk leads to action.

You can also use evidence. When your brain says, "I can't," ask, "What is one time I did something similar?" The answer does not have to be huge. Maybe you learned to ride a bike. Maybe you learned a new game. Evidence reminds your brain that you can learn.

Another inner-coach skill is how you talk to yourself after a mistake. Mistakes can teach you, or they can trap you. If you talk to yourself like an enemy, you will hide. If you talk to yourself like a teammate, you will repair and return.

Sometimes kids worry that kind self-talk is selfish. It is not. It is responsible. When you treat yourself with respect, you have more respect to give to others. A kid who lives in constant shame often becomes sharper and meaner because shame hurts.

Your inner coach also helps you handle judgment from outside. When someone says something unkind, your coach can answer, "That comment is not the full story of me." The coach can keep your identity steady while you decide what to do next.

If your inner critic is loud, start small. You do not need perfect self-talk. You need slightly better self-talk. Even one sentence like "I'm learning" can change how your body feels. And when your body feels steadier, your mind becomes clearer.

In a judgmental world, your inner coach is like a lantern you carry. It does not erase the darkness, but it helps you see your next step. With practice, that lantern becomes brighter, and your confidence becomes less dependent on anyone else's approval.

CHAPTER 29 - Bouncing Back

Some days go wrong. You get criticized. You lose a friend for a moment. You fail a quiz. You say something you regret. You feel embarrassed. In a judgmental world, a hard day can feel like proof that you are broken.

But a hard day is not your identity. It is a day. Resilience is the skill of returning to yourself after you are shaken. It does not mean you never fall. It means you learn how to stand again without losing your dignity.

The first part of bouncing back is allowing the feeling to exist without turning it into a life story. You can say, "Today hurt," without saying, "My whole life is terrible." Pain is real, but it does not get to write the whole book.

The second part is taking care of your body, because your body is where the emotions live. When you are hungry, tired, or overstimulated, everything feels bigger. A glass of water, food, a shower, movement, and sleep are not small things. They are emotional first aid.

The third part is choosing one honest sentence about what happened. Not a dramatic sentence, and not a denial. Just an honest one. For example: "I studied, but not in the right way." "I exploded because I was overwhelmed." Truth is the doorway to change.

Then comes repair. Repair is not punishment. Repair is responsibility. If you hurt someone, you can apologize without begging. A strong apology says what you did, why it was wrong, and what you will do differently next time. It is not a speech about how terrible you are. It is a plan to be better.

Sometimes the repair is with yourself. You may need to forgive yourself for being human. Forgiving yourself does not mean you approve of every choice. It means you refuse to live in endless shame. Shame keeps you stuck. Responsibility helps you move.

After repair, return to one small habit that steadies you. It might be cleaning your desk, taking a walk, practicing a skill, or doing one homework problem. Small order creates a feeling of control. It tells your brain, "We are back."

It also helps to share the hard day with a safe person. A trusted adult, a kind friend, or a caring coach can help you hold the story without drowning in it. You do not have to carry every emotion alone.

In a judgmental world, kids sometimes hide their hard moments because they fear being seen as weak. But hiding often makes pain grow. Sharing with the right person usually makes pain shrink.

Bouncing back also includes learning. Learning is not punishment either. It is power. You can ask, "What did today teach me?" Maybe it taught you to plan earlier, to speak more calmly, or to choose kinder friends. Lessons turn pain into progress.

There will be times when you bounce back quickly, and times when it takes longer. Taking longer does not mean you are failing. It means the hit was bigger. Give yourself time like you would give time to a sprained ankle.

In a judgmental world, people will sometimes remember your worst moment and act like it is the only thing about you. But you are not your worst moment. You are the person who learns from it. That learning is what makes you resilient, and resilience is one of the clearest forms of confidence.

CHAPTER 30 - Your Bright Future Map

You have reached the final chapter, but your growth is not ending. It is beginning in a new way. A book can give you tools, but you are the person who turns tools into a life.

In a judgmental world, it is easy to believe confidence is something you either have or you don't. But confidence is more like a skill. Skills are built through practice, mistakes, and returns. That means confidence belongs to you, not to luck and not to other people's opinions.

Across this book, you have met a set of steady ideas. You learned to step out of the comparison trap by measuring progress instead of people. You learned the difference between perfectionism and excellence so you can work hard without being cruel to yourself. You learned how to use your voice, how to handle being left out, and how to follow your values like a North Star.

In these last chapters, you learned to handle feedback without collapsing, to stay steady under pressure, to train an inner coach, and to bounce back after hard days. If you remember only one thing, let it be this: confidence grows when you return to yourself again and again.

A bright future is not built in one dramatic day. It is built in ordinary moments. It is built when you tell the truth, take the next step, and treat yourself with respect while you learn.

Your future map does not need to be perfect. It needs to be honest. An honest map includes your strengths and your struggles. It includes your people, your habits, and your values. It also includes your ability to change the map when you learn something new.

When the world judges you, return to three anchors. First: your values. Second: your effort. Third: your next step. Values keep you pointed in the right direction. Effort keeps you moving. Next step keeps you from freezing. Anchors do not remove storms, but they keep you from drifting.

You will still have days when you doubt yourself. That is normal. Even confident people have doubts. The difference is what they do next. They do not treat doubt like a stop sign. They treat it like a weather report. Weather changes. So do feelings.

When you feel small, remember that you are allowed to be a beginner. You are allowed to be in progress. You are allowed to ask for help. These permissions are not excuses. They are the foundation of growth.

Your confidence will also grow through relationships. Choose people who help you become clearer, not smaller. Choose friends who can tell the truth without humiliation. Choose adults who care more about your character than your score. The right people do not demand you shrink to fit them.

If you want a simple way to continue after this book, think of confidence as a daily practice of three kinds of courage. The courage to learn, even when you might fail. The courage to speak, even when your voice shakes. And the courage to be kind to yourself, even when you are disappointed.

One day, you will look back and realize you did not become confident by winning every battle. You became confident by building yourself into someone you can trust. That trust is the quiet strength that carries you through school, friendships, challenges, and dreams.

In a judgmental world, your life does not have to be a performance. It can be a journey. And you have something powerful for that journey: a mind that can learn, a heart that can heal, and a future that can be shaped by your choices.

Keep going. Keep learning. Keep returning to your best self. Your bright, full future is not waiting for you to be perfect. It is waiting for you to be real.